Roadside view of historic Hanalei Valley with its rainbow lei.

Rays of sunlight find one of the many magnificent waterfalls in Waimea Canyon.

Kilauea Lighthouse stands as a silent sentinel amidst this fish and wildlife refuge.

At left, Lumahai Beach, considered by many as one the of world's best, is surrounded by tropical splendor.
Above, snorkelers discover one more aspect of Lumahai Beach: an underwater fantasy.

*Above, golfers enjoy the quiet calm surrounding the 16th hole of the Kiele Course
at the entrance of Nawiliwili Bay.
At right, thundering surf along Kauai's south coast creates an atmosphere of drama and majesty.*

Clouds shroud rugged canyons laced with waterfalls on Mt. Waialeale.

Fern Grotto

At left, brightly clad scarecrows stand out in marked contrast to the surrounding lush greens of this Hanalei taro field.

Above, sugar mill composition.

Bougainvillaea ablaze, Hanapepe, Kauai.

Just a few of the reasons Kauai is the Garden Isle.

At left, flat-bottom boat plys the Wailua River, the only "river" in Hawaii while above, Wailua Falls contributes to the island's natural beauty.

At left, Waimea Canyon, Grand Canyon of the Pacific.

Above, visitors take in the super-sized spectacle from a canyon-rim lookout.

Above, Kalalau Beach on the Na Pali Coast.
At right, a stormy history etched in stone.

At times a visit to Nā Pali Coast, left, gives one the feeling of having reached the end of the earth.
Above, a lone weather station perched atop the southern end of the Nā Pali Coast.

At left, Menehune Fishpond, whose origin remains a mystery.
Above, rocky remnants of a Kaulu Paoa Heiau near Haena Beach.

Bali Hai: some like it cool!

Polihale: some like it hot!

Kauai in the sun, Spouting Horn

Kauai in the shade, Hanalei Bay

At left, heaven and earth come together in quiet pastoral symphony, while above, the brilliance of the setting sun silhouettes Niihau and Lehua Islands in a dramatic display of magenta magic.

Late afternoon over the Na Pali Coast, above, marks the beginning of a dazzling interplay of light combining land, sea and sky which culminates at dusk, at right, in a climax of breathtaking splendor.